JUST **3** STEPS

\

JUST 3 STEPS

Love Food ® is an imprint of
Parragon Books Ltd

Parragon
Queen Street House
4 Queen Street
Bath BA1 1HE, UK

Design: Terry Jeavons & Company
Additional photography: Clive Bozzard-Hill
Home economists: Valerie Barrett and
Carol Tennant
Introduction and additional recipes:
Christine McFadden

ISBN 978-1-4075-3387-2

Printed in China

This book uses metric and imperial
measurements. Follow the same units of
measurement throughout; do not mix metric
and imperial. All spoon measurements are
level, unless otherwise stated: teaspoons
are assumed to be 5ml, and tablespoons
are assumed to be 15ml. Unless otherwise
stated, milk is assumed to be full fat, eggs
and individual fruits, such as bananas, are
medium, and pepper is freshly ground
black pepper.

Recipes using raw or very lightly cooked eggs
should be avoided by children, the elderly,
pregnant women, convalescents, and anyone
suffering from an illness. Pregnant and
breast-feeding women are advised to avoid
eating peanuts and peanut products.

Contents

Introduction

If you don't always have the time or inclination to cook but love good food, this is the book for you. From start to finish, every recipe can be made in just three simple steps, whether it's a midweek meal or a special-occasion dinner, a solitary supper or a feast for friends.

There are no long lists of ingredients or elaborate instructions to overwhelm you and the recipes are clear and concise, and written in a logical step-by-step order. The ingredients lists are laid out in an easy-to-read format, are broken down into smaller sections where necessary, and can be used as a checklist for the store cupboard or a trip to the shops. Some of the ingredients need simple advance preparation, but once that's out of the way the recipes couldn't be simpler. Even the more time-consuming dishes can be made in only three steps and are just as quick to prepare and as hassle free as the speedier dishes – many of them can be left to marinate or simmer away for an hour or two while you get on with something more interesting.

It's a good idea to spend a little time getting organized before you start cooking to make meal preparation even easier.

- Read the recipe all the way through, making a note of any soaking, chilling or marinating stages.

- Assemble the pans and utensils you're going to need – that way you won't be frantically looking for something when the dish you're cooking needs urgent attention.

- Gather together all the ingredients before you start to cook.

- Make sure your knives are sharp. Get in the habit of passing the blade over a sharpener each time you use it, so you can chop and slice cleanly and quickly.

- Clear up as you go along.

With your utensils and ingredients assembled, you can relax and enjoy the actual process of easy three-step cooking. You'll be amazed by the sheer variety of dishes that can be produced this way – from tasty salads and soups to impressive meat, poultry or fish main courses. There are inspiring dishes for vegetarians that are sure to tempt most palates, and also a chapter devoted to fabulous desserts.

1 Light Bites

If you're short of time and need something simple to eat, these recipes are the answer. They show you how to rustle up a variety of mouth-watering but quickly prepared dishes in just three steps. From sustaining soups to substantial salads, and from pizza and bruschetta to sandwiches and wraps, these tasty light meals and snacks will keep you going at any time of day or night.

Chunky Vegetable Soup

INGREDIENTS

serves 6

2 carrots, sliced

1 onion, diced

1 garlic clove, crushed

350 g/12 oz new potatoes, diced

2 celery sticks, sliced

115 g/4 oz closed-cup mushrooms, quartered

400 g/14 oz canned chopped tomatoes

600 ml/1 pint vegetable stock

1 bay leaf

1 tsp dried mixed herbs

85 g/3 oz sweetcorn kernels, frozen or canned, drained

55 g/2 oz green cabbage, shredded

pepper

1 Put the carrots, onion, garlic, potatoes, celery, mushrooms, tomatoes and stock into a large saucepan. Stir in the bay leaf and herbs. Bring to the boil, then reduce the heat, cover and simmer for 25 minutes.

2 Add the sweetcorn and cabbage and return to the boil. Reduce the heat, cover and simmer for 5 minutes, or until the vegetables are tender. Remove and discard the bay leaf. Season to taste with pepper.

3 Ladle into warmed bowls and serve immediately.

Leek & Potato Soup

INGREDIENTS

55 g/2 oz butter

1 onion, chopped

3 leeks, sliced

225 g/8 oz potatoes, cut into 2-cm/¾-inch cubes

850 ml/1½ pints vegetable stock

150 ml/5 fl oz single cream (optional)

salt and pepper

fresh flat-leaf parsley sprigs, to garnish

crusty bread, to serve

serves ❹ to ❻

1 Melt the butter in a large saucepan over a medium heat, add the onion, leeks and potatoes and sauté gently for 2–3 minutes, until soft but not brown. Pour in the stock, bring to the boil, then reduce the heat and simmer, covered, for 15 minutes.

2 Remove from the heat and liquidize the soup in the saucepan using a hand-held stick blender if you have one. Alternatively, pour into a blender, liquidize until smooth and return to the rinsed-out saucepan.

3 Heat the soup, season to taste with salt and pepper and serve in warmed bowls. Swirl with the cream, if using, garnish with parsley and serve with crusty bread.

Chicken Noodle Soup

INGREDIENTS

2 skinless, boneless chicken breasts

1.2 litres/2 pints water or chicken stock

3 carrots, cut into 5-mm/ ¼-inch slices

85 g/3 oz vermicelli (or other small noodles)

salt and pepper

fresh tarragon leaves, to garnish

serves ❹ to ❻

1 Place the chicken in a large saucepan, add the water and bring to a simmer. Cook for 25–30 minutes. Skim any scum from the surface, if necessary. Remove the chicken from the liquid and keep warm.

2 Continue to simmer the liquid, add the carrots and vermicelli, and cook for 4–5 minutes.

3 Thinly slice or shred the chicken and place in warmed serving dishes. Season the soup to taste with salt and pepper and pour over the chicken. Garnish with the tarragon and serve immediately.

Pear & Roquefort Open Sandwiches

INGREDIENTS

serves ❷

4 slices walnut bread, about
1 cm/½ inch thick

4 thin slices cured ham,
such as **Bayonne** or **Parma**

2 ripe pears, halved, cored
and thinly sliced lengthways

100 g/3½ oz Roquefort
cheese, very thinly sliced

1 Preheat the grill to high. Put the bread slices under the grill and toast until crisp, but not brown, on both sides. Do not turn off the grill.

2 Fold or cut the ham slices to cover each slice of bread, then equally divide the pear slices between them. Lay the cheese slices on top.

3 Return the open sandwiches to the grill until the cheese melts and bubbles. Serve immediately.

Mushroom Fajitas

INGREDIENTS

serves ❹

2 tbsp oil

500 g/1 lb 2 oz large flat mushrooms, sliced

1 onion, sliced

1 red pepper, deseeded and sliced

1 green pepper, deseeded and sliced

1 garlic clove, crushed

¼–½ tsp cayenne pepper

juice and grated rind of 2 limes

2 tsp sugar

1 tsp dried oregano

8 flour tortillas

salt and pepper

salsa and lime wedges, to serve

1 Heat the oil in a large heavy-based frying pan. Add the mushrooms, onion, red and green peppers and garlic and stir-fry for 8–10 minutes, until the vegetables are cooked.

2 Add the cayenne pepper, lime juice and rind, sugar and oregano. Season to taste with salt and pepper and cook for a further 2 minutes.

3 Meanwhile, heat the tortillas according to the packet instructions. Divide the mushroom mixture between the warmed tortillas, roll up and serve with the salsa and lime wedges.

Nachos

INGREDIENTS

175 g/6 oz tortilla chips

400 g/14 oz canned refried beans, warmed

2 tbsp finely chopped bottled jalapeño chillies

200 g/7 oz canned or bottled pimientos or roasted peppers, drained and finely sliced

115 g/4 oz Gruyère cheese, grated

115 g/4 oz Cheddar cheese, grated

salt and pepper

guacamole and soured cream, to serve

serves 6

1 Preheat the oven to 200°C/400°F/Gas Mark 6. Spread the tortilla chips out over the base of a large, shallow ovenproof dish or roasting tin.

2 Cover the tortilla chips with the warmed refried beans. Sprinkle over the chillies and pimientos and season to taste with salt and pepper. Mix the cheeses together in a bowl and sprinkle on top.

3 Bake in the preheated oven for 5–8 minutes, until the cheese is bubbling and melted. Serve immediately with guacamole and soured cream.

Brunch Bruschetta

INGREDIENTS

serves ❷

4 slices ciabatta bread

1 large ripe tomato, diced

2 spring onions, finely sliced

1 small fresh buffalo
mozzarella cheese, diced

½ ripe avocado, diced

½ tbsp balsamic vinegar

2 tbsp extra virgin olive oil

salt and pepper

2 tbsp shredded fresh basil
leaves, to garnish

1 Preheat the grill to medium. Place the ciabatta on the rack in the grill pan. Grill until lightly browned, then turn and cook on the other side. Reserve and keep warm.

2 Mix the tomato, spring onions, mozzarella cheese, avocado, balsamic vinegar and half of the oil together in a medium bowl. Season to taste with salt and pepper.

3 Drizzle the remaining oil over the ciabatta toast and top with the tomato mixture. Garnish with the basil and serve immediately.

Ham & Pineapple Muffin Pizzas

INGREDIENTS

serves **4**

4 muffins

125 ml/4 fl oz ready-made tomato pizza sauce

2 sun-dried tomatoes in oil, drained and chopped

55 g/2 oz Parma ham

2 rings canned pineapple, chopped

½ green pepper, deseeded and chopped

125 g/4½ oz mozzarella cheese, cubed

olive oil, for drizzling

salt and pepper

1 Preheat the grill to medium. Cut the muffins in half and toast the cut side lightly under the preheated grill.

2 Spread the tomato sauce evenly over the muffins. Sprinkle the sun-dried tomatoes on top of the tomato sauce. Cut the Parma ham into thin strips and place on the muffins with the pineapple and green pepper. Carefully arrange the mozzarella cubes on top.

3 Drizzle a little oil over each pizza and season to taste with salt and pepper. Place under the preheated grill and cook until the cheese melts and bubbles. Serve immediately.

Chorizo & Cheese Quesadillas

INGREDIENTS

serves ❹

115 g/4 oz mozzarella cheese, grated

115 g/4 oz Cheddar cheese, grated

225 g/8 oz cooked chorizo sausage (outer casing removed), diced

4 spring onions, finely chopped

2 green chillies, deseeded and finely chopped

8 flour tortillas

vegetable oil, for brushing

salt and pepper

guacamole and salsa, to serve

1 Place the cheeses, chorizo, spring onions, chillies and salt and pepper to taste in a bowl and mix together. Divide the mixture between 4 of the flour tortillas, then top with the remaining tortillas.

2 Brush a large non-stick or heavy-based frying pan with oil and heat over a medium heat. Add 1 quesadilla and cook, pressing it down with a spatula, for 4–5 minutes, until the underside is crisp and lightly browned. Turn over and cook the other side until the cheese is melting. Remove from the frying pan and keep warm. Cook the remaining quesadillas.

3 Cut each quesadilla into quarters, arrange on a warmed serving plate and serve with guacamole and salsa.

Chicken Wraps

INGREDIENTS

serves 4

150 g/5½ oz natural yogurt

1 tbsp wholegrain mustard

280 g/10 oz cooked skinless, boneless chicken breast, diced

140 g/5 oz iceberg lettuce, finely shredded

85 g/3 oz cucumber, thinly sliced

2 celery sticks, sliced

85 g/3 oz black seedless grapes, halved

8 flour tortillas

pepper

1 Combine the yogurt and mustard in a bowl and season to taste with pepper. Stir in the chicken and toss until thoroughly coated.

2 Put the lettuce, cucumber, celery and grapes into a separate bowl and mix well.

3 Fold a tortilla in half and in half again to make a cone that is easy to hold. Half-fill the tortilla pocket with the salad mixture and top with some of the chicken mixture. Repeat with the remaining tortillas, salad and chicken. Serve immediately.

Raisin Coleslaw & Tuna-filled Pitta Breads

INGREDIENTS

serves ❹

85 g/3 oz grated carrot

55 g/2 oz white cabbage, thinly sliced

85 g/3 oz natural yogurt

1 tsp cider vinegar

25 g/1 oz raisins

200 g/7 oz canned tuna steak in water, drained

2 tbsp pumpkin seeds

4 pitta breads

pepper

4 dessert apples, to serve

1 Mix the carrot, cabbage, yogurt, vinegar and raisins together in a bowl. Lightly stir in the tuna and half the pumpkin seeds and season to taste with pepper.

2 Lightly toast the pitta breads under a preheated hot grill or in a toaster, then leave to cool slightly. Using a sharp knife, cut each pitta bread in half.

3 Divide the filling evenly between the pitta breads and sprinkle the remaining pumpkin seeds over the filling. Core the apples and cut into wedges, then serve immediately with the filled pitta breads.

Greek Salad

INGREDIENTS

4 tomatoes, cut into wedges

1 onion, sliced

½ cucumber, sliced

225 g/8 oz olives, stoned

**225 g/8 oz feta cheese, cubed
(drained weight)**

2 tbsp fresh coriander leaves

**fresh flat-leaf parsley
sprigs, to garnish**

pitta bread, to serve

DRESSING

5 tbsp extra virgin olive oil

2 tbsp white wine vinegar

1 tbsp lemon juice

½ tsp sugar

**1 tbsp chopped fresh
coriander**

salt and pepper

serves ❹

1 To make the dressing, place the oil, vinegar, lemon juice, sugar and coriander in a large bowl. Season to taste with salt and pepper and mix together well.

2 Place the tomatoes, onion, cucumber, olives, feta cheese and coriander in a bowl and pour over the dressing.

3 Toss all the ingredients together, then divide between individual serving bowls. Garnish with parsley sprigs and serve with pitta bread.

Roasted Vegetable Salad

INGREDIENTS

1 onion

1 aubergine

1 red pepper, deseeded

1 orange pepper, deseeded

1 large courgette

2–4 garlic cloves

2–4 tbsp olive oil

1 tbsp balsamic vinegar

2 tbsp extra virgin olive oil

1 tbsp shredded fresh basil

salt and pepper

Parmesan cheese shavings, to serve

serves ❹

1 Preheat the oven to 200°C/400°F/Gas Mark 6. Cut all the vegetables into even-sized wedges, put into a roasting tin and scatter over the garlic. Pour over 2 tablespoons of the olive oil and toss the vegetables until well coated with the oil. Season to taste with salt and pepper. Roast in the preheated oven for 40 minutes, or until tender, adding the extra olive oil if needed.

2 Meanwhile, put the vinegar, extra virgin olive oil and salt and pepper to taste into a screw-top jar and shake until blended.

3 Once the vegetables are cooked, remove from the oven, arrange on a serving dish and pour over the dressing. Sprinkle with the basil and serve with Parmesan cheese shavings.

Steak Waldorf Salad

INGREDIENTS

serves ❹

2 fillet steaks, about 175 g/ 6 oz each and 2.5 cm/1 inch thick

olive oil or sunflower oil, for brushing

1 tbsp wholegrain mustard

150 ml/5 fl oz mayonnaise

1 tbsp lemon juice

500 g/1 lb 2 oz eating apples

4 celery sticks, thinly sliced

70 g/2½ oz walnut halves, broken into pieces

100 g/3½ oz mixed salad leaves

pepper

crusty bread, to serve

1 Heat a cast-iron griddle pan or heavy-based frying pan over a medium heat. Brush each steak with oil and season to taste with pepper. Add the steaks to the pan and cook for 6–7 minutes for rare or 8–10 minutes for medium, turning the steaks frequently and brushing once or twice with oil. Remove from the pan and reserve.

2 Meanwhile, stir the mustard into the mayonnaise. Put the lemon juice into a large bowl. Peel and core the apples, then cut them into small chunks and immediately toss them in the lemon juice. Stir in the mustard mayonnaise. Add the celery and walnuts to the apple mixture and toss together.

3 Arrange the salad leaves on 4 plates, then divide the apple mixture between them. Very thinly slice the steaks, arrange on top of the salad and serve immediately with crusty bread.

Smoked Salmon, Asparagus & Avocado Salad

INGREDIENTS

200 g/7 oz fresh asparagus spears

1 large ripe avocado

1 tbsp lemon juice

large handful fresh rocket leaves

225 g/8 oz smoked salmon

1 red onion, finely sliced

1 tbsp chopped fresh parsley

1 tbsp snipped fresh chives

salt

DRESSING

1 garlic clove, chopped

4 tbsp extra virgin olive oil

2 tbsp white wine vinegar

1 tbsp lemon juice

pinch of sugar

1 tsp mustard

serves 4

1 Bring a large saucepan of lightly salted water to the boil. Add the asparagus and cook for 4 minutes, then drain. Refresh under cold running water and drain again. Set aside to cool.

2 To make the dressing, combine all the ingredients in a small bowl and stir together well. Cut the avocado in half lengthways, then remove and discard the stone and skin. Cut the flesh into bite-sized pieces and brush with lemon juice to prevent discoloration.

3 To assemble the salad, arrange the rocket leaves on individual serving plates and top with the asparagus and avocado. Cut the smoked salmon into strips and scatter over the top of the salad, then scatter over the onion and herbs. Drizzle over the dressing and serve.

2 Meat

With its appetizing flavour and texture, meat is an all-time favourite. Take your pick from richly flavoured beef, sweet and delicate lamb or tasty pork and gammon. There is a wonderful choice of cooking methods that will bring out the best in the meat you have bought. The recipes here include speedy stir-fries and grills, succulent roasts, homely meat loaf and tasty pasta dishes, as well as leisurely stews and braises that take care of themselves while cooking.

Grilled Steak with Tomatoes & Garlic

INGREDIENTS

3 tbsp olive oil, plus extra for brushing

700 g/1 lb 9 oz tomatoes, peeled and chopped

1 red pepper, deseeded and chopped

1 onion, chopped

2 garlic cloves, finely chopped

1 tbsp chopped fresh flat-leaf parsley

1 tsp dried oregano

1 tsp sugar

4 entrecôte steaks or rump steaks, about 175 g/6 oz each

salt and pepper

cooked green beans and new potatoes, to serve

serves ❹

1 Place the oil, tomatoes, red pepper, onion, garlic, parsley, oregano and sugar in a heavy-based saucepan and season to taste with salt and pepper. Bring to the boil, reduce the heat and simmer for 15 minutes.

2 Meanwhile, preheat the grill to high or preheat a griddle pan over a high heat. Snip any fat around the outsides of the steaks. Season each generously with pepper and brush with oil. Cook for 1 minute on each side, then reduce the heat to medium and cook according to taste: 1½–2 minutes each side for rare; 2½–3 minutes each side for medium; 3–4 minutes on each side for well done.

3 Transfer the steaks to warmed individual plates with the sauce. Serve immediately with green beans and new potatoes.

The Best Steak Burgers

INGREDIENTS

serves 4

500 g/1 lb 2 oz fresh steak mince

½ small onion, very finely chopped or grated (optional)

vegetable oil, for brushing

salt and pepper

TO SERVE

4 hamburger buns

lettuce leaves

sliced gherkins (optional)

tomato relish or other sauce of your choice

1 Place the steak mince in a bowl, add the onion, if using, and season to taste with salt and pepper. Mix well together, divide into 4 portions and shape each into a round patty, about 2.5 cm/½ inch thick.

2 Preheat the grill to medium–high. Brush the burgers with oil and cook under the preheated grill, turning once, for 8–12 minutes, until browned and cooked through.

3 Meanwhile, split the hamburger buns in half and place the lettuce leaves on the bottom halves. Put a cooked burger on top of each and add the gherkins, if using, and tomato relish. Top with the remaining hamburger bun halves and serve immediately.

Thick Beef & Button Onion Casserole

INGREDIENTS

serves 6

2 tbsp olive oil

450 g/1 lb button onions,
peeled but kept whole

2 garlic cloves, halved

900 g/2 lb stewing beef,
cubed

½ tsp ground cinnamon

1 tsp ground cloves

1 tsp ground cumin

2 tbsp tomato purée

750 ml/1¼ pints red wine

grated rind and juice of
1 orange

1 bay leaf

salt and pepper

1 tbsp chopped fresh flat-
leaf parsley, to garnish

mashed potatoes, to serve

1 Preheat the oven to 150°C/300°F/Gas Mark 2. Heat the oil in a large flameproof casserole and cook the whole onions and garlic, stirring frequently, for 5 minutes, or until soft and beginning to brown. Add the beef and cook over a high heat, stirring frequently, for 5 minutes, or until browned on all sides.

2 Stir the spices and tomato purée into the casserole and season to taste with salt and pepper. Pour in the wine, scraping any sediment from the base of the casserole, then add the orange rind and juice, and the bay leaf. Bring to the boil and cover.

3 Cook in the preheated oven for about 2 hours. Remove the lid and cook the casserole for a further hour, stirring once or twice, until the meat is tender. Remove from the oven, garnish with the parsley and serve hot with mashed potatoes.

Beef & Red Wine Pot Roast

INGREDIENTS

serves 6

1.6 kg–1.8 kg/3 lb 8 oz–4 lb rolled beef silverside or brisket

3 tbsp vegetable oil

1 onion, finely chopped

2 celery sticks, finely diced

2 carrots, finely diced

1 fresh bay leaf

1 heaped tsp dried thyme

150 ml/5 fl oz meat stock

300–350 ml/10–12 fl oz red wine

½ tbsp plain flour, plus extra for dusting

salt and pepper

1 Preheat the oven to 150°C/300°F/Gas Mark 2. Season the meat well with salt and pepper and dust with flour. Heat the oil in a flameproof casserole in which the meat fits snugly. Cook the meat on all sides until browned and transfer to a plate. Add the onion, celery and carrots to the casserole and cook until soft.

2 Return the meat to the casserole and add the bay leaf, thyme, stock and enough wine to come one third of the way up the meat. Bring to the boil, cover tightly with a lid and place in the preheated oven. Cook for 3–3½ hours, turning occasionally, and topping up the liquid, if necessary. Transfer the meat to a warmed serving platter and cover loosely with foil.

3 Using kitchen paper, remove any excess fat from the surface of the liquid in the casserole. Strain the remaining liquid into a saucepan and bring to the boil, adding any juices from the meat. Mix the flour to a thin paste with a little water and whisk into the liquid to thicken. Check the seasoning and adjust, if necessary. Pour a little of the sauce over the meat and serve the remainder in a jug.

Hot & Spicy Beef with Toasted Pine Kernels

INGREDIENTS

serves ❹

3 tbsp soy sauce

1½ tbsp cornflour

450 g/1 lb rump steak

55 g/2 oz pine kernels

juice of 1 lime

2 tbsp white wine vinegar

2 tbsp groundnut oil

3 tsp grated fresh ginger

2 red chillies, finely chopped

4 baby leeks, halved

2 carrots, thinly sliced

100 g/3½ oz fine tip asparagus

3 shallots, thinly sliced

cooked noodles, to serve

1 Mix 2 tablespoons of the soy sauce with 1 tablespoon of the cornflour and 1 tablespoon of cold water in a medium bowl. Cut the beef into thin strips, then add to the bowl and stir until the meat is well coated. Cover with clingfilm and chill in the refrigerator for 1 hour. Preheat the grill to medium. Spread the pine kernels on a baking sheet and toast under the preheated grill. Set aside.

2 Mix the lime juice, vinegar, the remaining cornflour and soy sauce, and 1 tablespoon of the oil in a small bowl and set aside. Heat the remaining oil in a large frying pan or wok. Stir-fry the ginger, chillies and leeks for 2 minutes. Add the beef mixture and stir-fry for a further minute.

3 Stir in the carrots, asparagus and shallots and stir-fry for 7 minutes, or until the beef is cooked through. Add the lime mixture, reduce the heat and simmer until the liquid thickens. Remove from the heat, sprinkle with the reserved pine kernels and serve with cooked noodles.

Meatloaf

INGREDIENTS

1 thick slice white bread, crusts removed

700 g/1 lb 9 oz fresh beef, pork or lamb mince

1 small egg

1 tbsp finely chopped onion

1 beef stock cube, crumbled

1 tsp dried mixed herbs

salt and pepper

TO SERVE

sauce or gravy

mashed potatoes

cooked runner beans

serves ❹

1 Preheat the oven to 180°C/350°F/Gas Mark 4. Put the bread into a small bowl and add enough water to soak. Leave to stand for 5 minutes, then drain and squeeze well to remove the water. Crumble the bread into small pieces.

2 Combine the bread with the meat, egg, onion, stock cube and herbs in a bowl and season to taste with salt and pepper. Shape into a loaf, then place on a baking sheet or in an ovenproof dish.

3 Bake the meatloaf in the preheated oven for 30–45 minutes, until the juices run clear when it is pierced with a skewer. Cut into slices and serve with sauce, mashed potatoes and runner beans.

Minted Lamb Chops

INGREDIENTS

serves ❹

6 lamb chump chops, about
175 g/6 oz each

150 ml/5 fl oz Greek-style
yogurt

2 garlic cloves, finely
chopped

1 tsp grated fresh ginger

¼ tsp coriander seeds,
crushed

1 tbsp olive oil, plus extra
for brushing

1 tbsp orange juice

1 tsp walnut oil

2 tbsp chopped fresh mint

salt and pepper

1 Place the chops in a large, shallow non-metallic bowl. Mix half the yogurt, the garlic, ginger and coriander seeds in a jug and season to taste with salt and pepper. Spoon the mixture over the chops, turning to coat, then cover with clingfilm and leave to marinate in the refrigerator for 2 hours, turning occasionally.

2 Preheat the barbecue or grill. Place the remaining yogurt, the olive oil, orange juice, walnut oil and mint in a small bowl and whisk until thoroughly blended. Season to taste with salt and pepper. Cover with clingfilm and leave to chill in the refrigerator until ready to serve.

3 Drain the chops, scraping off the marinade. Brush with olive oil and cook over medium–hot coals or under the preheated grill for 5–7 minutes on each side. Serve immediately with the minted yogurt.

Tagine of Lamb

INGREDIENTS

serves 4

350 g/12 oz boneless lamb

1 tbsp sunflower oil

1 onion, chopped

1 garlic clove, chopped

600 ml/1 pint stock

grated rind and juice of 1 orange

1 tsp clear honey

1 cinnamon stick

1-cm/½-inch piece fresh ginger, finely chopped

1 aubergine

4 tomatoes, peeled and chopped

115 g/4 oz dried apricots

2 tbsp chopped fresh coriander

salt and pepper

cooked couscous, to serve

1 Trim all visible fat from the lamb and cut into 2.5-cm/1-inch cubes. Heat the oil in a large heavy-based frying pan or flameproof casserole over a medium heat. Add the onion and lamb and cook, stirring frequently, for 5 minutes, or until the meat is lightly browned all over. Add the garlic, stock, orange rind and juice, honey, cinnamon stick and ginger. Bring to the boil, then reduce the heat, cover and leave to simmer for 45 minutes.

2 Using a sharp knife, halve the aubergine lengthways and slice thinly. Add to the frying pan with the tomatoes and apricots. Cover and cook for a further 45 minutes, or until the lamb is tender.

3 Stir in the coriander and season to taste with salt and pepper. Serve immediately with cooked couscous.

Caramelized Lamb Shanks with Root Vegetables

INGREDIENTS

serves 4

4 tbsp clear honey

1 tbsp vegetable oil

1 tsp dried thyme or oregano

2 tsp pepper

½ tsp salt

4 lamb shanks, about
400 g/14 oz each

350–500 ml/12–18 fl oz stock

1 head garlic, unpeeled,
sliced in half across the
centre

1 onion, quartered

1 parsnip, quartered
lengthways

4 small salad potatoes,
halved lengthways

4 small carrots

1 Preheat the oven to 180°C/ 350°F/Gas Mark 4. Mix together the honey, oil, thyme, pepper and salt, and rub all over the lamb shanks. Place the lamb shanks in a roasting tin with 200 ml/ 7 fl oz of the stock, the garlic and onion.

2 Cook in the preheated oven for 1 hour, turning the lamb after 30 minutes. Turn again, and add the parsnip, potatoes, carrots and 150 ml/5 fl oz of the remaining stock. Cook for a further 30 minutes and turn the lamb again. Add a little more stock, if necessary, then cook for a further 15 minutes.

3 Using a slotted spoon, transfer the meat and vegetables to a warmed serving dish. Using kitchen paper, remove any excess fat from the surface of the liquid in the tin. Place the tin over a medium heat and stir for a few seconds, until the liquid is syrupy. Pour over the meat and vegetables, and serve immediately.

Glazed Gammon Steaks

INGREDIENTS

serves ❹

4 gammon steaks

4 tbsp dark brown sugar

2 tsp mustard powder

4 tbsp butter

8 rings canned pineapple

1 Preheat a griddle pan over a medium heat. Place the gammon steaks in it and cook for 5 minutes, turning once. If you only have room for 2 steaks at a time, cook them completely and keep warm while cooking the second pair.

2 Combine the brown sugar and mustard in a small bowl. Melt the butter in a large frying pan. Add the pineapple and cook for 2 minutes to heat through, turning once. Sprinkle with the sugar and mustard mixture and continue cooking over a low heat until the sugar has melted and the pineapple is well glazed. Turn the pineapple once more so that both sides are coated with sauce.

3 Place the gammon steaks on individual plates and top each with 2 pineapple rings. Spoon over the pan juices and serve.

Pork Chops with Rosemary & White Bean Mash

INGREDIENTS

serves **2**

2 thick pork loin chops, about 300–350g/10½–12 oz each

olive oil, for brushing

generous knob of butter

1 garlic clove, crushed

1 tsp finely chopped fresh rosemary, plus extra sprigs to garnish

400 g/14 oz canned cannellini beans, drained and rinsed

salt and pepper

1 Season the pork chops well with salt and pepper and brush with oil. Heat a non-stick heavy-based pan over a medium heat. Cook the chops for 5 minutes on each side, until browned. Reduce the heat, cover the pan and cook for another 10–15 minutes, depending on thickness, turning once.

2 Meanwhile, heat the butter with the garlic and chopped rosemary in a small pan over a medium heat. Add all but 3 tablespoons of the beans and moisten with 2 tablespoons of water. Stir to heat through, then mash to a coarse purée with the back of a wooden spoon. Season to taste with salt and pepper.

3 Divide the mashed beans between 2 warmed plates. Top each with a pork chop and pour over the pan juices. Briefly warm the reserved whole beans, then scatter over the chops. Garnish with rosemary sprigs and serve.

Roasted Pork Fillet with Fennel

INGREDIENTS

serves ❷ to ❸

**1 pork fillet, about 550–600g/
1 lb 4 oz–1 lb 5 oz**

3 tbsp olive oil

1½ tsp fennel seeds

1 large garlic clove

**1½ tsp finely chopped fresh
rosemary**

¾ tsp sea salt

¾ tsp pepper

2 tsp balsamic vinegar

**2 fennel bulbs, trimmed and
very thinly sliced**

125 ml/4 fl oz stock

1 Make slits all over the pork with a sharp knife. Rub with 1 tablespoon of the oil. In a mortar, grind the fennel seeds, garlic, rosemary, salt and pepper to a coarse paste with a pestle. Push about two thirds of the paste into the slits in the pork. Mix together the vinegar, remaining oil and remaining paste in a bowl, add the fennel and toss to mix. Leave to marinate for 30 minutes.

2 Preheat the oven to 220°C/425°F/Gas Mark 7. Place the pork and fennel in a shallow roasting tin, add the stock and cook in the preheated oven for 10 minutes. Reduce the heat to 190°C/375°F/Gas Mark 5, and roast for a further 10–15 minutes, stirring occasionally.

3 Transfer the pork to a warmed serving dish, cover loosely with foil and leave to rest for 15 minutes in a warm place. Meanwhile, return the roasting tin with the fennel to the switched-off oven. Carve the meat into thick diagonal slices and top with the fennel and any juices from the tin.

Spaghetti alla Carbonara

INGREDIENTS

serves ❹

450 g/1 lb dried spaghetti

1 tbsp olive oil

225 g/8 oz rindless pancetta
or streaky bacon, chopped

4 eggs

5 tbsp single cream

4 tbsp freshly grated
Parmesan cheese

salt and pepper

1 Bring a large heavy-based saucepan of lightly
salted water to the boil. Add the pasta, return to
the boil and cook for 8–10 minutes, or until
tender but still firm to the bite.

2 Meanwhile, heat the oil in a heavy-based frying
pan. Add the pancetta and cook over a medium
heat, stirring frequently, for 8–10 minutes.

3 Beat the eggs with the cream in a small bowl
and season to taste with salt and pepper. Drain
the pasta and return it to the saucepan. Tip in the
contents of the frying pan, then add the egg
mixture and half the Parmesan cheese. Stir well,
then transfer to a warmed serving dish. Serve
immediately, sprinkled with the remaining cheese.

3 Poultry

Whether it's a simple roast chicken, a juicy pan-fried duck breast or a spicy turkey stir-fry, poultry is one of the most good-tempered and versatile foods. It combines perfectly with a wide spectrum of tasty ingredients, offering endless inspiration for delicious meals. As the recipes in this chapter show, you can create curries and casseroles, roasts and stir-fries, or burgers and grills in just three easy steps.

Chicken Pepperonata

INGREDIENTS

serves ❹

8 skinless chicken thighs

2 tbsp wholemeal flour

2 tbsp olive oil

1 small onion, thinly sliced

1 garlic clove, crushed

1 each large red, yellow and green pepper, deseeded and thinly sliced

400 g/14 oz canned chopped tomatoes

1 tbsp chopped fresh oregano, plus extra to garnish

salt and pepper

crusty wholemeal bread, to serve

1 Toss the chicken thighs in the flour, shaking off the excess. Heat the oil in a wide frying pan and cook the chicken quickly until sealed and lightly browned, then remove from the pan.

2 Add the onion to the pan and cook gently until soft. Add the garlic, peppers, tomatoes and oregano, then bring to the boil, stirring.

3 Arrange the chicken over the vegetables, season well with salt and pepper, then cover the pan tightly and simmer for 20–25 minutes, or until the chicken is completely cooked and tender. Garnish with oregano and serve with crusty wholemeal bread.

Tarragon Chicken

INGREDIENTS

serves ❹

4 skinless, boneless chicken breasts, about 175 g/6 oz each

125 ml/4 fl oz dry white wine

225–300 ml/8–10 fl oz chicken stock

1 garlic clove, finely chopped

1 tbsp dried tarragon

175 ml/6 fl oz double cream

1 tbsp chopped fresh tarragon

salt and pepper

cooked runner beans, to serve

1 Season the chicken well with salt and pepper and place in a single layer in a large heavy-based frying pan. Pour in the wine and enough chicken stock just to cover and add the garlic and dried tarragon. Bring to the boil, reduce the heat and cook gently for 10 minutes, or until the chicken is tender and cooked through.

2 Remove the chicken with a slotted spoon, cover and keep warm. Strain the poaching liquid through a sieve into a clean frying pan and skim off any fat from the surface. Bring to the boil and cook for 12–15 minutes, or until reduced by about two thirds.

3 Stir in the cream, return to the boil and cook until reduced by about half. Stir in the fresh tarragon. Arrange the chicken on warmed serving plates, spoon over the sauce and serve immediately with cooked runner beans.

Thai Red Chicken Curry

INGREDIENTS

6 garlic cloves, chopped

2 red chillies, chopped

2 tbsp chopped lemon grass

1 tsp finely grated lime rind

1 tbsp chopped lime leaves

1 tbsp Thai red curry paste

1 tbsp coriander seeds

1 tbsp chilli oil

4 skinless, boneless chicken breasts, sliced

300 ml/10 fl oz coconut milk

300 ml/10 fl oz chicken stock

1 tbsp soy sauce

55 g/2 oz ground peanuts

3 spring onions, sliced

1 red pepper, deseeded and sliced

3 Thai aubergines, sliced

chopped fresh coriander, to garnish

cooked rice, to serve

serves ❷ to ❹

1 Place the garlic, chillies, lemon grass, lime rind, lime leaves, curry paste and coriander seeds in a food processor and process until the mixture is smooth.

2 Heat the oil in a preheated wok or large frying pan over a high heat. Add the chicken and the garlic mixture and stir-fry for 5 minutes. Add the coconut milk, stock and soy sauce and bring to the boil. Reduce the heat and cook, stirring, for a further 3 minutes. Stir in the ground peanuts and simmer for 20 minutes.

3 Add the spring onions, red pepper and aubergines and leave to simmer, stirring occasionally, for a further 10 minutes. Garnish with coriander and serve with cooked rice.

Chicken Fried Rice

INGREDIENTS

serves 4

½ tbsp sesame oil

6 shallots, quartered

450g/1 lb cooked chicken, diced

3 tbsp soy sauce

2 carrots, diced

1 celery stick, diced

1 red pepper, deseeded and diced

175g/6 oz fresh peas

100 g/3½ oz canned sweetcorn, drained

275 g/9½ oz cooked long-grain rice

2 large eggs, scrambled

1 Heat the oil in a large frying pan over a medium heat. Add the shallots and cook until soft, then add the chicken and 2 tablespoons of the soy sauce and stir-fry for 5–6 minutes.

2 Stir in the carrots, celery, red pepper, peas and sweetcorn and stir-fry for a further 5 minutes. Add the rice and stir thoroughly.

3 Finally, stir in the scrambled eggs and the remaining soy sauce. Serve immediately.

Chicken Satay

INGREDIENTS

2 tbsp vegetable oil or
groundnut oil

1 tbsp sesame oil

juice of ½ lime

2 skinless, boneless chicken
breasts, cut into small cubes

crushed peanuts, to garnish

DIP

2 tbsp vegetable oil or
groundnut oil

1 small onion, finely chopped

1 small green chilli,
deseeded and chopped

1 garlic clove, finely chopped

125 ml/4 fl oz crunchy peanut
butter

6–8 tbsp water

juice of ½ lime

serves ❹

1 Combine both the oils and the lime juice in a
non-metallic dish. Add the chicken cubes,
cover with clingfilm and chill for 1 hour.

2 To make the dip, heat the oil in a frying pan
and cook the onion, chilli and garlic over a low
heat, stirring occasionally, for about 5 minutes,
until just softened. Add the peanut butter,
water and lime juice and simmer gently, stirring
constantly, until the peanut butter has softened
enough to make a dip – you may need to add
extra water to make a thinner consistency.

3 Preheat the barbecue or grill. Drain the chicken
cubes and thread them onto 8–12 presoaked
wooden skewers. Cook over hot coals or under
the preheated grill, turning frequently, for
about 10 minutes, until cooked through and
browned. Serve hot with the warm dip,
garnished with crushed peanuts.

Paprika Chicken with Soured Cream

INGREDIENTS

serves 4

1 tbsp butter

2 tbsp vegetable oil

1 onion, sliced

2 green peppers, deseeded
and chopped

1 tbsp paprika

1.5 kg/3 lb 5 oz chicken
thighs and drumsticks

200 ml/7 fl oz stock

150 ml/5 fl oz soured cream

1 tsp plain flour

salt and pepper

1 tbsp snipped fresh dill,
to garnish

cooked rice, to serve

1 Heat the butter and 1 tablespoon of the oil in a pan and cook the onion and green peppers until soft. Stir in the paprika and season to taste with salt and pepper. Cook for a further 5 minutes, stirring occasionally.

2 Meanwhile, heat the remaining oil in a lidded flameproof casserole dish or heavy-based saucepan and cook the chicken pieces until browned all over. Add the onion and pepper mixture and the stock. Cover tightly and simmer over a low heat for 45 minutes. Remove the lid and cook for a further 15 minutes.

3 Remove the pan from the heat and remove any excess fat from the surface using kitchen paper. Return to a medium–low heat, then gradually stir in the soured cream and the flour. Simmer gently for 3–4 minutes, stirring, until thickened. Check and adjust the seasoning, if necessary, sprinkle with the dill and serve with cooked rice.

Roast Chicken with Cumin Butter & Preserved Lemon

INGREDIENTS

100 g/3½ oz butter, softened

½ tbsp cumin seeds, lightly crushed

½ preserved lemon, finely chopped

1 large garlic clove, crushed

1 whole chicken, about 1.5 kg/3 lb 5 oz

salt and pepper

roasted vegetables, to serve

serves ❸ to ❹

1 Preheat the oven to 220°C/425°F/Gas Mark 7. Mash together the butter, cumin seeds, preserved lemon and garlic, and season to taste with salt and pepper. Using your fingers, loosen the skin on the chicken breasts and legs. Push most of the flavoured butter under the skin, moulding it to the shape of the bird. Smear any remaining butter over the skin.

2 Place the chicken in a roasting tin and cook in the preheated oven for 20 minutes. Reduce the temperature to 180°C/350°F/Gas Mark 4 and cook for a further 50–55 minutes, until the juices run clear when you pierce the thickest part of the chicken with a skewer. Transfer the chicken to a warmed serving dish, cover loosely with foil and leave to rest for 15 minutes.

3 Pour off most of the fat from the roasting tin. Place the tin over a medium heat and cook the juices for a few minutes, scraping any sediment from the base of the tin, until reduced slightly. Carve the chicken into slices, pour over the juices and serve with roasted vegetables.

Turkey Escalopes with Green Peppercorn Sauce

INGREDIENTS

serves 4

1 tbsp vegetable oil

25 g/1 oz butter

2 shallots, chopped

700 g/1 lb 9 oz lb turkey
escalopes, cut into thin
strips

225 g/8 oz button
mushrooms, sliced

300 ml/10 fl oz soured cream

1 tbsp green peppercorns in
brine, drained

finely grated rind of ½ lemon

salt and pepper

snipped fresh chives,
to garnish

1 Heat the oil and butter in a large heavy-based frying pan, add the shallots and cook until softened. Add the turkey and cook over a medium–high heat until golden. Remove the turkey from the pan with a slotted spoon and keep warm.

2 Add the mushrooms to the pan and cook for 5 minutes, stirring, until softened. Return the turkey to the pan and season to taste with salt and pepper. Stir in the soured cream, peppercorns and lemon rind, and warm through gently.

3 Transfer to a warmed serving dish, garnish with chives and serve.

Lemon & Mint Turkey Burgers

INGREDIENTS

serves ❹

500 g/1 lb 2 oz fresh turkey mince

½ small onion, grated

finely grated rind and juice of 1 small lemon

1 garlic clove, finely chopped

2 tbsp finely chopped fresh mint

½ tsp pepper

1 tsp sea salt

1 egg, beaten

1 tbsp olive oil, plus extra for frying

lemon wedges, to serve

1 Place all the ingredients in a bowl and mix well with a fork. Shape the mixture into 12 balls rolling them with the palm of your hand. Flatten into patties about 2 cm/¾ inch thick. Cover and leave in the refrigerator for at least 1 hour, or overnight.

2 Heat about 5 tablespoons of oil in a large heavy-based frying pan. When the oil starts to look hazy add the burgers, cooking in batches if necessary. Cook over a medium–high heat for 4–5 minutes on each side, until golden brown and cooked through.

3 Drain the burgers on kitchen paper and transfer to a warmed serving dish. Serve with lemon wedges.

Turkey & Cashew Nut Stir-fry

INGREDIENTS

serves ❹

1 tbsp cornflour

½ tsp five-spice powder

4 turkey steaks, cut into
thin strips

1 tsp soy sauce

1 tsp dry sherry

3 tbsp groundnut oil

1 garlic clove, finely
chopped

2.5-cm/1-inch piece fresh
ginger, finely chopped

4 spring onions, cut into thin
strips

1 large carrot, cut into thin
strips

85 g/3 oz cashew nuts

2 tbsp hoisin sauce

½ tsp salt

shredded spring onion,
to garnish

cooked rice, to serve

1 Mix together the cornflour and five-spice powder in a bowl and stir in the turkey. Add the soy sauce and sherry, stirring to coat. Set aside for 30 minutes.

2 Heat a wok or large frying pan over a high heat. Heat 2 tablespoons of the oil, then add the turkey mixture and stir-fry for 2–3 minutes, until golden and cooked through. Using a slotted spoon, transfer the turkey to a plate and keep warm.

3 Heat the remaining oil in the wok and stir-fry the garlic, ginger, spring onions and carrot for 1 minute. Return the turkey to the wok with the cashew nuts, hoisin sauce and salt. Reduce the heat to medium–high and stir-fry for a further minute. Sprinkle with shredded spring onion and serve immediately with cooked rice.

Balsamic-glazed Duck Breasts

INGREDIENTS

serves ❹

4 duck breasts with skin, about 200 g/7 oz each

4 tbsp stock

2 tbsp ready-made balsamic glaze or balsamic vinegar

salt and pepper

cooked green beans and sautéed potatoes, to serve

1 Preheat the oven to 220°C/425°F/Gas Mark 7. Slash the skin on each duck breast a few times with a sharp knife and rub well with salt and pepper.

2 Heat an ovenproof frying pan over a medium–high heat. Cook the duck breasts skin-side down for 3–4 minutes. Transfer the pan to the preheated oven and cook for a further 5 minutes. Turn the duck breasts and cook for a further 5 minutes. Transfer to a warmed serving dish and leave to rest for at least 10 minutes.

3 Pour off any excess fat from the frying pan and stir in the stock over a medium heat. Add the balsamic glaze and the juices from the duck. Simmer for a few seconds, until the liquid is syrupy. Cut the duck breasts into thick diagonal slices, pour over the sauce and serve with cooked green beans and sautéed potatoes.

Roast Duck Legs with Pears & Ginger

INGREDIENTS

4 duck legs

2 firm pears, quartered, cored and peeled

2 onions, quartered lengthways

cooked noodles, to serve

MARINADE

1 tbsp grated fresh ginger

juice of 1 lemon

4 tbsp clear honey

2 tbsp soy sauce

2 tbsp toasted sesame oil

pepper

serves 4

1 Combine the marinade ingredients in a shallow dish. Add the duck legs, toss in the marinade and leave in the refrigerator for at least 2 hours, or overnight.

2 Preheat the oven to 180°C/350°F/Gas Mark 4. Arrange the pear and onion quarters in the bottom of a small roasting tin with a rack. Pour in all but 4 tablespoons of the marinade. Place the duck legs on the rack and cook in the preheated oven for 40 minutes, brushing the duck with the reserved marinade. Turn over the duck and cook for a further 15 minutes.

3 Transfer the duck legs, pears and onions to a warmed serving dish. Drain off most of the fat from the tin. Place the tin over a medium–high heat and briefly simmer the remaining liquid, stirring. Pour the sauce over the duck legs and serve with cooked noodles.

4 Fish & Seafood

Fish and seafood are so simple to cook that they are the perfect candidates for cooking in just three steps. Straightforward techniques make the most of their natural tenderness and clean fresh flavours. Grilling, stir-frying or shallow-frying, or just a quick roasting at a high temperature, are all that's needed to produce delectable results. Whatever cooking method you choose, make sure to use the freshest fish possible.

Salmon Steaks with Parsley Pesto

INGREDIENTS

serves ❹

**4 salmon steaks, about
175 g/6 oz each**

**griddled lemon wedges,
to garnish**

fresh rocket, to serve

PARSLEY PESTO

**2 garlic cloves, roughly
chopped**

25 g/1 oz pine kernels

**40 g/1½ oz fresh parsley,
coarse stems removed**

1 tsp salt

**25 g/1 oz freshly grated
Parmesan cheese**

**125–150 ml/4–5 fl oz extra
virgin olive oil**

1 To make the parsley pesto, put the garlic, pine kernels, parsley and salt into a food processor and blend to a purée. Add the Parmesan and blend briefly again. Add 125 ml/4 fl oz of the oil and blend again. If the consistency is too thick, add the remaining oil and blend again until smooth. Scrape into a bowl and set aside.

2 Meanwhile, preheat the grill to medium. Cook the salmon under the preheated grill for 10–15 minutes, depending on the thickness of the fillets, until the flesh turns pink and flakes easily.

3 Transfer the salmon to individual serving plates. Garnish with lemon wedges and serve with the parsley pesto and rocket.

Salmon Fingers with Potato Wedges

INGREDIENTS

serves ❷ to ❸

150 g/5 oz fine cornmeal or polenta

1 tsp paprika

400 g/14 oz salmon fillet, skinned and sliced into 12 chunky fingers

1 egg, beaten

sunflower oil, for frying

POTATO WEDGES

500 g/1 lb 2 oz potatoes, scrubbed and cut into thick wedges

1–2 tbsp olive oil

½ tsp paprika

salt

1 Preheat the oven to 200°C/400°F/Gas Mark 6. To make the potato wedges, dry the potatoes on a clean tea towel. Spoon the oil into a roasting tin and put into the preheated oven briefly to heat. Toss the potatoes in the warm oil until well coated. Sprinkle with paprika and salt to taste and roast for 30 minutes, turning halfway through, until crisp and golden.

2 Meanwhile, mix the cornmeal and paprika together on a plate. Dip each salmon finger into the beaten egg, then roll in the cornmeal mixture until evenly coated.

3 Heat enough oil to cover the base of a large heavy-based frying pan over a medium heat. Carefully arrange half the salmon fingers in the pan and cook for 6 minutes, turning halfway through, until golden. Drain on kitchen paper and keep warm while you cook the remaining salmon fingers. Serve with the potato wedges.

Tuna with a Chilli Crust

INGREDIENTS

1 small bunch fresh coriander or flat-leaf parsley

3–4 dried red chillies, crushed

2 tbsp sesame seeds

1 egg white

4 tuna steaks, about 140–175 g/5–6 oz each

2–3 tbsp sunflower oil

salt and pepper

lime wedges, to garnish

serves ❹

1 Chop the coriander, leaving a few leaves whole to garnish. Mix the crushed chillies, chopped coriander and sesame seeds together in a shallow dish and season to taste with salt and pepper. Lightly beat the egg white with a fork in a separate shallow dish.

2 Dip the tuna steaks first in the egg white, then in the chilli and herb mixture to coat. Gently pat the crust evenly over the fish with the palm of your hand, making sure that both sides of the steaks are well covered.

3 Heat the oil in a large heavy-based frying pan. Add the tuna and cook over a medium heat for 4 minutes, then turn over carefully, using a fish slice. Cook for a further 4 minutes, then transfer to warmed serving plates. Garnish with the lime wedges and the reserved coriander leaves, and serve immediately.

Spaghetti with Tuna & Parsley

INGREDIENTS

serves 6

500 g/1 lb 2 oz dried
spaghetti

25 g/1 oz butter

200 g/7 oz canned tuna,
drained and flaked

55 g/2 oz canned anchovies,
drained

250 ml/9 fl oz olive oil

1 large bunch fresh
flat-leaf parsley, roughly
chopped

150 ml/5 fl oz crème fraîche

salt and pepper

1 Bring a large heavy-based saucepan of
lightly salted water to the boil. Add the
spaghetti, return to the boil and cook for
8–10 minutes, or until tender but still firm
to the bite. Drain the spaghetti in a colander
and return to the saucepan. Add the butter,
toss thoroughly to coat and keep warm
until required.

2 Place the tuna in a food processor or blender
with the anchovies, oil and parsley and process
until the sauce is smooth. Pour in the crème
fraîche and process for a few seconds to blend.
Taste the sauce and season with salt and
pepper, if necessary.

3 Shake the saucepan of spaghetti over a
medium heat for a few minutes, or until it is
thoroughly warmed. Pour the sauce over the
spaghetti and toss quickly. Serve immediately.

Grilled Trout Fillets

INGREDIENTS

serves 4

2 tbsp chopped toasted hazelnuts

2 tbsp ground almonds

115 g/4 oz Cheddar cheese, grated

4 tbsp fresh breadcrumbs, white or wholemeal

1 egg

1 tbsp milk

4 brown trout fillets, about 175 g/6 oz each

2 tbsp plain flour

salt and pepper

1 Preheat the grill to medium. Place the hazelnuts and almonds in a large bowl. Add the cheese and breadcrumbs and mix together. Place the egg and milk in a separate bowl and beat together. Season to taste with salt and pepper.

2 Rinse the fish fillets and pat dry with kitchen paper. Coat the fillets in the flour, then dip them into the egg mixture. Transfer them to the bowl containing the nuts and cheese, and turn the fillets in the mixture until thoroughly coated.

3 Cook the fish under the preheated grill for 5 minutes, turning once during the cooking time, or until golden and cooked through. Remove from the grill and transfer to warmed plates. Serve immediately.

Monkfish Stir-fry

INGREDIENTS

serves ❹

2 tsp sesame oil

450 g/1 lb monkfish steaks,
cut into 2.5-cm/1-inch
chunks

1 onion, thinly sliced

3 garlic cloves, finely
chopped

1 tsp grated fresh ginger

225 g/8 oz fine tip asparagus

175 g/6 oz mushrooms, thinly
sliced

2 tbsp soy sauce

1 tbsp lemon juice

1 Heat the oil in a frying pan over a medium–high
heat. Add the monkfish, onion, garlic, ginger,
asparagus and mushrooms. Stir-fry for
2–3 minutes.

2 Stir in the soy sauce and lemon juice and
cook for another minute.

3 Remove from the heat and transfer to
warmed serving dishes. Serve immediately.

Sea Bass with Fennel Butter

INGREDIENTS

serves ❷

2 small sea bass, about 350g/12 oz each, scaled, gutted and heads removed

2 tsp fennel seeds, crushed

3 tbsp flour

1 tbsp vegetable oil

125 g/4½ oz butter

juice of ½ lemon

1 tbsp finely chopped fresh flat-leaf parsley

salt and pepper

lemon wedges, to garnish

1 Slash the sea bass in 2–3 places on each side. Stuff half the fennel seeds into the slits. Dredge the fish in the flour.

2 Heat the oil and 25 g/1 oz of the butter in a heavy-based non-stick frying pan over a medium–high heat. Cook the fish for 1½ minutes each side, until browned. Season generously with salt and pepper, and sprinkle over the lemon juice. Reduce the heat to medium, cover the pan and cook for 5 minutes, then turn and cook for a further 2–3 minutes, until the flesh is opaque.

3 Transfer the fish to warmed serving plates. Wipe out the pan with kitchen paper, add the remaining butter and fennel seeds, and cook over a medium–high heat, until golden and foaming. Pour over the fish, sprinkle with the parsley and serve immediately, garnished with the lemon wedges.

Pan-fried Halibut Steaks with Tomato Salsa

INGREDIENTS

serves ❹

1 tbsp vegetable oil

50 g/1¾ oz butter

4 halibut steaks, about
2.5 cm/1 inch thick

flour, for dusting

juice of ½ lemon

salt and pepper

TOMATO SALSA

3 firm tomatoes, halved,
deseeded and finely diced

1 small red onion, finely
diced

1 green chilli, deseeded and
finely chopped

3 tbsp chopped fresh
coriander

juice of 1 lime

½ tsp sea salt

1 Combine all the salsa ingredients in a serving bowl and leave to stand at room temperature.

2 Heat the oil and 40 g/1½ oz of the butter in a large frying pan over a medium–high heat. Dust the halibut steaks with flour and season to taste with salt and pepper. Place in the pan and cook for 5 minutes on one side and 3–4 minutes on the other, until golden and cooked through. Transfer to a warmed serving dish.

3 Add the lemon juice to the pan and simmer over a medium heat for a few seconds, scraping up any sediment from the base of the pan. Stir in the remaining butter and cook for a few seconds. Pour over the fish and serve immediately with the salsa.

Barbecued Mackerel

INGREDIENTS

4 mackerel

2 tbsp olive oil

2 tbsp lemon juice

sea salt and pepper

lemon wedges and cooked green beans, to serve

serves ❹

1 Clean and gut the fish and remove the heads. Make diagonal slashes on each side of the flesh. Rub all over with the oil, lemon juice, sea salt and pepper, pushing the salt and pepper well into the slashes.

2 Preheat the barbecue or grill. Cook over hot coals or under the preheated grill for 5–6 minutes on each side.

3 Transfer to warmed plates and serve with lemon wedges and cooked green beans.

Linguine with Anchovies, Olives & Capers

INGREDIENTS

serves 4

3 tbsp olive oil

2 garlic cloves, finely chopped

10 anchovy fillets, drained and chopped

140 g/5 oz black olives, stoned and chopped

1 tbsp capers, rinsed

450 g/1 lb plum tomatoes, peeled, deseeded and chopped

pinch of cayenne pepper

400 g/14 oz dried linguine

salt

2 tbsp chopped fresh flat-leaf parsley, to garnish

1 Heat the oil in a heavy-based saucepan. Add the garlic and cook over a low heat, stirring frequently, for 2 minutes. Add the anchovies and mash them to a pulp with a fork. Add the olives, capers and tomatoes, and season to taste with cayenne pepper. Cover and simmer for 25 minutes.

2 Meanwhile, bring a saucepan of lightly salted water to the boil. Add the pasta, bring back to the boil and cook for 8–10 minutes, until tender but still firm to the bite. Drain and transfer to a warmed serving dish.

3 Spoon the anchovy sauce into the dish and toss the pasta, using 2 large forks. Garnish with the parsley and serve immediately.

Prawn & Lime Kebabs

INGREDIENTS

serves **4**

20 raw tiger prawns

1 red onion, cut into 2.5-cm/
1-inch chunks

½ yellow and ½ red pepper,
deseeded and cut into
2.5-cm/1-inch chunks

lime wedges, to garnish

cooked rice and lime and
ginger chutney, to serve

MARINADE

6 tbsp lime juice

finely grated rind of 1 lime

2 tbsp olive oil

1 garlic clove, crushed

1 green chilli, deseeded and
thinly sliced

2 tsp finely chopped fresh
flat-leaf parsley

salt and pepper

1 Peel the prawns, leaving the tails intact. Cut a slit along the back of each prawn, then remove and discard the dark vein.

2 Place the marinade ingredients in a screw-top jar and shake well. Place the prawns in a shallow dish and the onion and pepper chunks in a separate dish. Divide the marinade between the two dishes, tossing the prawns and vegetables to coat. Cover and leave in the refrigerator for at least 1 hour.

3 Preheat the barbecue or grill. Thread the ingredients onto four metal or presoaked wooden skewers, alternating the prawns and vegetables. Cook over hot coals or under the preheated grill for 10 minutes, turning occasionally. Garnish with lime wedges and serve with cooked rice and chutney.

Mussel & Potato Gratin

INGREDIENTS

serves ❹

600 g/1 lb 5oz live mussels, scrubbed and debearded

1 large onion, thinly sliced

400 g/14 oz canned chopped tomatoes

450 g/1lb new potatoes, thinly sliced

3 tbsp chopped fresh flat-leaf parsley

2 garlic cloves, finely chopped

100 g/3½ oz pecorino cheese, coarsely grated

olive oil, for drizzling

100 g/3½ oz coarse stale breadcrumbs

salt and pepper

1 Discard any mussels with broken shells or any that refuse to close when tapped. Place in a saucepan with 225 ml/8 fl oz water and cook, covered, over a high heat for 3–4 minutes. Strain through a muslin-lined sieve, reserving the liquid. Discard any mussels that remain closed. Discard one half of each shell, and reserve the other half-shell containing the flesh.

2 Preheat the oven to 180°C/350°F/Gas Mark 4. Spread half the onion over the base of a 2-litre/3½-pint baking dish. Add half the tomatoes and half the potatoes then repeat the layers with the remaining onion, tomatoes and potatoes, sprinkling with the parsley and garlic, and seasoning well with salt and pepper. Top with one third of the pecorino cheese. Pour over 225 ml/8 fl oz of the mussel liquid and drizzle with oil.

3 Bake in the preheated oven for 40 minutes. Arrange the reserved mussels in their half-shells on top and sprinkle with the remaining cheese and the breadcrumbs. Increase the heat to 200°C/400°F/Gas Mark 6 and bake for a further 10 minutes, until golden. Serve immediately.

Seared Scallops & Leeks

INGREDIENTS

serves **4**

**4 thin leeks, halved
lengthways then crossways**

5 tbsp olive oil

20 large scallops

sea salt and pepper

**snipped fresh chives and
lemon wedges, to garnish**

1 Preheat the oven to 230°C/450°F/Gas Mark 8.
Arrange the leeks cut-side up in a single layer
in an ovenproof dish. Drizzle with 3 tablespoons
of the oil, then sprinkle with sea salt and
pepper, pushing it into the crevices. Cook in
the preheated oven for 8–10 minutes, until
brown at the edges but still bright green and
tender-crisp.

2 Score the scallops with criss-cross slashes.
Heat the remaining oil in a frying pan over a
high heat. Cook the scallops for 3–4 minutes,
until just browned but slightly translucent on
the inside.

3 Remove the leeks from the oven and arrange
on warmed serving plates with the scallops on
top. Simmer the scallop juices in the pan until
slightly reduced, then pour over the scallops
and leeks. Garnish with the chives and lemon
wedges, and serve immediately.

5 Vegetarian

Vegetarian meals are perfect for exploring the sheer variety of dishes that can be cooked in only three steps. By combining store cupboard ingredients with top-notch fresh vegetables, cheese or eggs, you can have colourful, flavour-packed dishes on the table in very little time at all. Many of the dishes in this chapter can be prepared ahead and reheated when you need them – perfect for a speedy supper or a lunch on the run.

Mushroom Stroganoff

INGREDIENTS

25 g/1 oz butter

1 onion, finely chopped

450 g/1 lb closed cup mushrooms, quartered

1 tsp tomato purée

1 tsp coarse grain mustard

150 ml/5 fl oz crème fraîche

1 tsp paprika, plus extra to garnish

salt and pepper

fresh flat-leaf parsley sprigs, to garnish

serves ❹

1 Heat the butter in a large heavy-based frying pan. Add the onion and cook gently for 5–10 minutes, until soft.

2 Add the mushrooms to the frying pan and stir-fry for a few minutes, until they begin to soften. Stir in the tomato purée and mustard, then add the crème fraîche. Cook gently, stirring constantly, for 5 minutes.

3 Stir in the paprika and season to taste with salt and pepper. Garnish with extra paprika and parsley sprigs, and serve immediately.

Bean & Vegetable Chilli

INGREDIENTS

serves **4**

4 tbsp vegetable stock

1 onion, roughly chopped

1 green pepper, deseeded and finely chopped

1 red pepper, deseeded and finely chopped

1 tsp finely chopped garlic

1 tsp finely chopped fresh ginger

2 tsp ground cumin

½ tsp chilli powder

2 tbsp tomato purée

400 g/14 oz canned chopped tomatoes

400 g/14 oz canned kidney beans, drained

400 g/14 oz canned black-eyed beans, drained

salt and pepper

corn tortillas, to serve

1 Heat the stock in a large saucepan, add the onion and peppers and simmer for 5 minutes, or until softened.

2 Stir in the garlic, ginger, cumin, chilli powder, tomato purée and tomatoes. Season to taste with salt and pepper and simmer for 10 minutes.

3 Stir in the beans and simmer for a further 5 minutes, or until hot. Remove the pan from the heat and transfer the chilli to a warmed serving dish. Serve with corn tortillas.

Linguine with Wild Mushroom & Mascarpone Sauce

INGREDIENTS

450 g/1 lb dried linguine

55 g/2 oz butter

1 garlic clove, crushed

225 g/8 oz mixed wild mushrooms, sliced

250 g/9 oz mascarpone cheese

2 tbsp milk

1 tsp chopped fresh sage, plus extra leaves to garnish

salt and pepper

Parmesan cheese shavings, to serve

serves ❹

1 Bring a large heavy-based saucepan of lightly salted water to the boil. Add the pasta, return to the boil and cook for 8–10 minutes, until tender but still firm to the bite.

2 Meanwhile, melt the butter in a separate large saucepan. Add the garlic and mushrooms and cook for 3–4 minutes. Reduce the heat and stir in the mascarpone cheese, milk and chopped sage. Season to taste with salt and pepper.

3 Drain the pasta thoroughly and add to the mushroom sauce. Toss until the pasta is well coated with the sauce. Transfer to warmed dishes, garnish with sage leaves and serve immediately with Parmesan cheese shavings.

Pasta with Basil & Pine Kernel Pesto

INGREDIENTS

about 40 fresh basil leaves

3 garlic cloves, crushed

25 g/1 oz pine kernels

50 g/1¾ oz finely grated Parmesan cheese, plus extra to serve

2–3 tbsp extra virgin olive oil

350 g/12 oz dried pasta

salt and pepper

serves ❹

1 Rinse the basil leaves and pat them dry with kitchen paper. Place the basil leaves, garlic, pine kernels and Parmesan cheese in a food processor and blend for 30 seconds, or until smooth. With the motor running, slowly add enough of the oil to reach the desired consistency. Season to taste with salt and pepper.

2 Bring a large heavy-based saucepan of lightly salted water to the boil. Add the pasta, return to the boil and cook for 8–10 minutes, until tender but still firm to the bite.

3 Drain the pasta thoroughly, then transfer to a serving plate and add the pesto. Toss well to mix and serve with extra grated Parmesan cheese.

Creamy Spinach & Mushroom Pasta

INGREDIENTS

serves ❹

300 g/10½ oz dried penne

2 tbsp olive oil

250 g/9 oz mushrooms, sliced

1 tsp dried oregano

250 ml/9 fl oz vegetable
stock

1 tbsp lemon juice

6 tbsp cream cheese

200 g/7 oz frozen spinach
leaves

salt and pepper

1 Bring a large heavy-based saucepan of lightly salted water to the boil. Add the pasta, return to the boil and cook for 8–10 minutes, until tender but still firm to the bite. Drain, reserving 175 ml/6 fl oz of the cooking liquid.

2 Meanwhile, heat the oil in a large heavy-based frying pan over a medium heat, add the mushrooms and cook, stirring frequently, for 8 minutes, or until almost crisp. Stir in the oregano, stock and lemon juice and cook for 10–12 minutes, or until the sauce is reduced by half.

3 Stir in the cream cheese and spinach and cook over a medium–low heat for 3–5 minutes. Add the reserved cooking liquid, then the cooked pasta. Stir well, season to taste with salt and pepper and heat through before serving.

Red Onion & Goat's Cheese Tartlets

INGREDIENTS

2 tbsp olive oil

4 red onions, halved and thinly sliced

2 tbsp balsamic vinegar

2 tbsp stock

1 tsp sugar

1 tsp fresh thyme leaves

200 g/7 oz ready-made shortcrust pastry

2 tbsp pine kernels

4 thin slices goat's cheese from a log

salt and pepper

serves ❹

1 Preheat the oven to 180°C/350°F/Gas Mark 4. Heat the oil in large heavy-based frying pan over a medium heat. Add the onions and cook gently for 15 minutes, stirring frequently. Stir in the vinegar, stock, sugar and thyme, and season to taste with salt and pepper. Cook, stirring, for a further 20 minutes.

2 Meanwhile, roll out the pastry and use to line four 12-cm/4½-inch tartlet tins. Line with foil and fill with baking beans. Bake blind in the preheated oven for 10 minutes. Remove the foil and beans.

3 Spread the onion mixture over the bases of the pastry cases. Sprinkle with the pine kernels and arrange the goat's cheese on top. Bake for 15 minutes, until the cheese is melted and starting to colour. Serve hot.

Baked Sweet Potatoes with Ginger & Coriander

INGREDIENTS

4 sweet potatoes, about 300 g/10½ oz each

vegetable oil, for brushing

50 g/1¾ oz butter

40 g/1½ oz fresh ginger, sliced into very thin matchsticks

2 tbsp chopped fresh coriander

salt and pepper

serves 4

1 Preheat the oven to 230°C/450°F/Gas Mark 8. Brush the sweet potatoes with oil and bake in the preheated oven for 40–45 minutes, until tender. Cut a cross in the top of each potato. Press the flesh upwards until it bursts through the cuts.

2 Heat the butter in a frying pan over a medium–high heat, until foaming. Add the ginger and cook for 3–4 minutes, until golden and crisp.

3 Pour the ginger and buttery juices over the potatoes. Sprinkle with the coriander, season to taste with salt and pepper, and serve.

Mangetout, Sesame & Tofu Stir-fry

INGREDIENTS

serves ❷ to ❸

2 tbsp toasted sesame oil

3 tbsp groundnut oil

200 g/7 oz small shiitake
mushrooms

2 heads pak choi, leaves left
whole, stalks sliced

150 g/5 oz mangetout, sliced
in half at an angle

250-g/9-oz pack tofu,
drained and cubed

3-cm/1¼-inch piece fresh
ginger, thinly sliced

2 garlic cloves, finely
chopped

1 tbsp soy sauce

1 tsp sesame seeds

salt and pepper

cooked noodles, to serve

1 Heat the oils in a wok over a high heat. Add the mushrooms, pak choi stalks and mangetout, and stir-fry for 1 minute.

2 Add the tofu, pak choi leaves, ginger, garlic and a splash of water to moisten. Stir-fry for a further 1–2 minutes, until the pak choi leaves have wilted.

3 Stir in the soy sauce, sprinkle with the sesame seeds and season to taste with salt and pepper. Serve immediately with cooked noodles.

Baked Peppers with Olives & Feta

INGREDIENTS

4 peppers, red and yellow, halved and deseeded

3 garlic cloves, crushed

1 tsp finely chopped fresh rosemary

1 tsp thyme leaves

85 g/3 oz coarse stale breadcrumbs

3 tbsp extra virgin olive oil

7 black olives, stoned

50 g/1¾ oz feta cheese, cut into 1-cm/½-inch cubes

salt and pepper

serves ❷

1 Preheat the oven to 240°C/475°F/Gas Mark 9. Place the peppers cut-side down in a shallow roasting tin. Cook in the preheated oven for 20 minutes, until the skin wrinkles and begins to blacken. Remove the tin from the oven, cover with a thick tea towel and leave for 5 minutes, then peel the skin off the peppers.

2 Reduce the oven temperature to 220°C/ 425°F/Gas Mark 7. Cut the peppers into bite-sized chunks and place in a shallow ovenproof dish. Combine the garlic, herbs and breadcrumbs in a small bowl. Season to taste with salt and pepper, and stir in the oil. Scatter the mixture over the peppers and top with the olives and feta cheese.

3 Place the dish in the preheated oven and bake for 10–15 minutes, until the breadcrumbs are crisp and the cheese is starting to colour.

Braised Borlotti Beans & Tomatoes with Parmesan Toasts

INGREDIENTS

serves 4

7 tbsp olive oil

10–12 fresh sage leaves, roughly chopped

1 red onion, thinly sliced

2 large garlic cloves, thinly sliced

400 g/14 oz canned chopped tomatoes

1 tbsp tomato purée

800 g/1 lb 12 oz canned borlotti beans, drained and rinsed

8 thin slices ciabatta bread

50 g/1¾ oz freshly grated Parmesan cheese

salt and pepper

1 Heat 5 tablespoons of the oil in a large heavy-based saucepan over a medium heat. Add the sage, onion and garlic and cook gently for 5 minutes. Stir in the tomatoes and the tomato purée and cook for a further 2–3 minutes, stirring.

2 Add the beans, cover and cook for 20 minutes, adding a little water if necessary – the mixture should be quite soupy. Season to taste with salt and pepper.

3 Preheat the grill to medium. Drizzle the remaining oil over the bread and sprinkle with the Parmesan cheese. Place under the preheated grill and cook for a few minutes, until the cheese is golden and bubbling. Divide the slices of toasted bread between 4 warmed serving dishes and spoon the bean mixture over the top. Serve immediately.

Spicy Fried Eggs

INGREDIENTS

serves **2**

2 tbsp olive oil

1 large onion, finely
chopped

2 green or red peppers,
deseeded and roughly
chopped

1 garlic clove, finely
chopped

½ tsp dried chilli flakes

4 plum tomatoes, peeled and
roughly chopped

2 eggs

1 tbsp chopped fresh
flat-leaf parsley

salt and pepper

1 Heat the oil in a large non-stick frying pan
over a medium heat. Add the onion and cook
until golden. Add the peppers, garlic and chilli
flakes and cook until the peppers are soft.

2 Stir in the tomatoes, season to taste with
salt and pepper and simmer over a medium–low
heat for 10 minutes.

3 Using the back of a spoon, make 2 depressions
in the mixture in the frying pan. Break the eggs
into the depressions, cover and cook for
3–4 minutes, until the eggs are set. Sprinkle
with the parsley and serve.

Puy Lentils Provençal

INGREDIENTS

serves 2

2 tbsp olive oil

1 courgette, quartered lengthways and sliced

1 red pepper, deseeded and diced

2 garlic cloves, crushed

150 g/5 oz cherry tomatoes

400 g/14 oz canned Puy lentils, drained

1 tsp red wine vinegar

pinch of dried chilli flakes

salt and pepper

1 Heat the oil in a heavy-based frying pan over a medium heat. Add the courgette, red pepper and garlic and cook for 5 minutes, until soft.

2 Add the tomatoes and crush with the back of a wooden spoon. Cook for a further 1–2 minutes.

3 Stir in the lentils and cook for 3–4 minutes to heat through. Add the vinegar and chilli flakes, season to taste with salt and pepper, and serve hot.

Spicy Chickpea & Aubergine Casserole

INGREDIENTS

1 tbsp cumin seeds

2 tbsp coriander seeds

2 tsp dried oregano or thyme

5 tbsp vegetable oil

2 onions, chopped

1 red pepper, deseeded and cut into 2-cm/¾-inch chunks

1 aubergine, cut into 2-cm/¾-inch chunks

2 garlic cloves, chopped

1 green chilli, chopped

400 g/14 oz canned chopped tomatoes

400 g/14 oz canned chickpeas, drained and rinsed

225 g/8 oz green beans, cut into 2-cm/¾-inch lengths

600 ml/1 pint stock

3 tbsp chopped fresh coriander

serves 6

1 Dry-fry the seeds in a heavy-based frying pan for a few seconds, until aromatic. Add the oregano and cook for a further few seconds. Remove from the heat, transfer to a mortar and crush with a pestle.

2 Heat the oil in a large heavy-based casserole dish. Cook the onions, red pepper and aubergine for 10 minutes, until soft. Add the ground seed mixture, garlic and chilli and cook for a further 2 minutes.

3 Add the tomatoes, chickpeas, green beans and stock. Bring to the boil, then cover and simmer gently for 1 hour. Stir in the coriander and serve immediately.

5 Sweet Treats

Desserts are a treat but we often don't have the time to make them. The recipes here show you that three steps are all it takes to concoct a creamy tiramisu or crème brûlée, a fragrant fruit compote or an irresistible cheesecake. There are also no-fuss recipes for flapjacks, gingerbread and chocolate chip biscuits – delicious snacks to have on hand when you're in the mood for something sweet.

Creamy Rice Pudding

INGREDIENTS

serves ❹

1 tbsp butter, for greasing

85 g/3 oz sultanas, plus extra to decorate

5 tbsp caster sugar

90 g/3¼ oz pudding rice

1.2 litres/2 pints milk

1 tsp vanilla extract

finely grated rind of 1 large lemon

pinch of freshly grated nutmeg

chopped pistachio nuts, to decorate

1 Preheat the oven to 160°C/325°F/Gas Mark 3. Grease an 850-ml/1½-pint ovenproof dish with butter.

2 Put the sultanas, sugar and rice into a mixing bowl, then stir in the milk and vanilla extract. Transfer to the prepared dish, sprinkle over the lemon rind and nutmeg, then bake in the preheated oven for 2½ hours.

3 Remove from the oven and transfer to individual serving bowls. Decorate with sultanas and chopped pistachio nuts and serve.

Cheat's Crème Brûlée

INGREDIENTS

225–300 g/8–10½ oz mixed soft fruits, such as blueberries, strawberries and raspberries

1½–2 tbsp Cointreau or orange flower water

250 g/9 oz mascarpone cheese

200 ml/7 fl oz crème fraîche

2–3 tbsp dark muscovado sugar

serves ❹ to ❻

1 Prepare the fruit, if necessary, and lightly rinse, then place in the bases of 4–6 x 150-ml/ 5-fl oz ramekin dishes. Sprinkle the fruit with the Cointreau.

2 Cream the mascarpone cheese in a bowl until soft, then gradually beat in the crème fraîche. Spoon the mascarpone mixture over the fruit, smoothing the surface and ensuring that the tops are level. Chill in the refrigerator for at least 2 hours.

3 Sprinkle the tops with the sugar. Using a chef's blow torch, grill the tops until caramelized (about 2–3 minutes). Alternatively, cook under a preheated grill, turning the dishes, for 3–4 minutes, or until the tops are lightly caramelized all over. Serve immediately or chill in the refrigerator for 15–20 minutes before serving.

Chocolate Mousse

INGREDIENTS

300 g/10½ oz plain chocolate

1½ tbsp unsalted butter

1 tbsp brandy

4 eggs, separated

serves ❹

1 Break the chocolate into small pieces and place in a heatproof bowl set over a pan of simmering water. Add the butter and melt with the chocolate, stirring, until smooth. Remove from the heat, stir in the brandy and leave to cool slightly. Add the egg yolks and beat until smooth.

2 In a separate bowl, whisk the egg whites until stiff peaks have formed, then fold into the chocolate mixture. Spoon into 4 small serving bowls and level the surfaces. Transfer to the refrigerator and chill for at least 4 hours until set.

3 Take the mousse out of the refrigerator and serve.

Tiramisu

INGREDIENTS

serves ❹

200 ml/7 fl oz strong black coffee, cooled to room temperature

4 tbsp orange liqueur, such as Cointreau

3 tbsp orange juice

16 Italian sponge fingers

250 g/9 oz mascarpone cheese

300 ml/10 fl oz double cream, lightly whipped

3 tbsp icing sugar

grated rind of 1 orange

60 g/2¼ oz plain dark chocolate, grated

chopped toasted almonds and strips of orange zest, to decorate

1 Pour the cooled coffee into a jug and stir in the orange liqueur and orange juice. Place 8 of the sponge fingers in the base of a serving dish, then pour over half of the coffee mixture.

2 Place the mascarpone cheese in a separate bowl together with the cream, icing sugar and orange rind, and mix well. Spread half of the mascarpone mixture over the coffee-soaked sponge fingers, then arrange the remaining sponge fingers on top. Pour over the remaining coffee mixture then spread over the remaining mascarpone mixture.

3 Scatter over the grated chocolate and leave to chill in the refrigerator for at least 2 hours. Serve decorated with chopped toasted almonds and strips of orange zest.

Deep Chocolate Cheesecake

INGREDIENTS

115 g/4 oz digestive biscuits, finely crushed

2 tsp cocoa powder

4 tbsp butter, melted, plus extra for greasing

chocolate leaves, to decorate

CHOCOLATE LAYER

800 g/1 lb 12 oz mascarpone cheese

200 g/7 oz icing sugar, sifted

juice of ½ orange

finely grated rind of 1 orange

175 g/6 oz plain dark chocolate, melted

2 tbsp brandy

serves ④ to ⑥

1 Grease a 20-cm/8-inch loose-based cake tin. To make the base, put the crushed biscuits, cocoa powder and melted butter into a large bowl and mix well. Press the biscuit mixture evenly over the base of the prepared tin.

2 Put the mascarpone cheese and icing sugar into a bowl and stir in the orange juice and rind. Add the melted chocolate and brandy and mix together until thoroughly combined. Spread the chocolate mixture evenly over the biscuit layer. Cover with clingfilm and chill for at least 4 hours.

3 Remove the cheesecake from the refrigerator, turn out onto a serving platter and decorate with chocolate leaves. Serve immediately.

Apple Strudel with Warm Cider Sauce

INGREDIENTS

8 eating apples

1 tbsp lemon juice

85 g/3 oz sultanas

1 tsp ground cinnamon

½ tsp grated nutmeg

1 tbsp soft light brown sugar

6 sheets filo pastry

vegetable oil spray

icing sugar, for dusting

CIDER SAUCE

1 tbsp cornflour

450 ml/16 fl oz cider

serves ❷ to ❹

1 Preheat the oven to 190°C/375°F/Gas Mark 5. Line a baking sheet with non-stick baking paper. Peel and core the apples and cut them into 1-cm/½-inch pieces. Toss the pieces in a bowl with the lemon juice, sultanas, cinnamon, nutmeg and sugar.

2 Lay out a sheet of filo pastry, spray with vegetable oil and lay a second sheet on top. Repeat with a third sheet. Spread over half the apple mixture and roll up lengthways, tucking in the ends to enclose the filling. Repeat to make a second strudel. Slide onto the baking sheet, spray with oil and bake in the preheated oven for 15–20 minutes.

3 Meanwhile, to make the sauce, blend the cornflour in a saucepan with a little of the cider until smooth. Add the remaining cider and heat gently, stirring constantly, until the mixture boils and thickens. Serve the strudel warm or cold, dusted with icing sugar and accompanied by the cider sauce.

Dark Plum Compote

INGREDIENTS

600 g/1 lb 5 oz dark-skinned plums, halved and stoned

lightly whipped cream or crème fraîche, to serve

SYRUP

150 g/5 oz sugar

400 ml/14 fl oz water

3 fresh bay leaves, torn

1 thinly pared strip of orange zest

serves ❹

1 Place the plum halves in a serving bowl.

2 Place the syrup ingredients in a saucepan. Stir over a medium heat until the sugar has dissolved, then boil for 7–10 minutes, until syrupy. Immediately strain the boiling syrup over the plums. Leave to cool to room temperature.

3 Serve the plum compote with lightly whipped cream.

Basil-scented Strawberries & Nectarines

INGREDIENTS

500 g/1 lb 2 oz strawberries, hulled

1 tbsp lemon juice

2 ripe nectarines, halved and stoned

10–12 basil leaves, torn

2 tbsp sugar

serves ❹

1 Slice the strawberries, if they are large, and place in a bowl with the lemon juice.

2 Slice each of the nectarine halves lengthways into three segments. Slice each segment in half crossways and add to the bowl.

3 Crush the basil with the sugar using a mortar and pestle. Add to the fruit and mix well. Leave to stand for 30 minutes. Serve at room temperature.

Gingerbread Squares

INGREDIENTS

90 g/3¼ oz butter or margarine, plus extra for greasing

55 g/2 oz muscovado sugar

5 tbsp black treacle

1 egg white

1 tsp almond extract

175 g/6 oz plain flour, plus extra for dusting

¼ tsp bicarbonate of soda

¼ tsp baking powder

pinch of salt

½ tsp mixed spice

½ tsp ground ginger

125 g/4½ oz dessert apples, finely chopped, cooked

makes ❷❹

1 Preheat the oven to 180°C/350°F/Gas Mark 4. Grease a large baking sheet and line it with baking paper. Put the butter, sugar, treacle, egg white and almond extract into a food processor and blend until smooth.

2 In a separate bowl, sift the flour, bicarbonate of soda, baking powder, salt, mixed spice and ginger together. Add to the creamed mixture and beat together thoroughly. Stir in the chopped apples. Pour the mixture onto the prepared baking tray.

3 Transfer to the preheated oven and bake for 10 minutes, or until golden brown. Remove from the oven and cut into 24 pieces. Transfer the squares to a wire rack and let them cool completely before serving.

Chocolate Chip Biscuits

INGREDIENTS

215 g/7½ oz plain flour, sifted

1 tsp baking powder

115 g/4 oz soft margarine, plus extra for greasing

125 g/4½ oz light brown sugar

50 g/1¾ oz caster sugar

½ tsp vanilla extract

1 egg

115 g/4 oz plain chocolate chips

makes 18

1 Preheat the oven to 190°C/375°F/Gas Mark 5. Place all the ingredients in a large mixing bowl and beat until they are thoroughly combined.

2 Lightly grease 2 baking sheets. Place 9 tablespoonfuls of the mixture onto each baking sheet, spacing them well apart to allow for spreading during cooking.

3 Bake in the preheated oven for 10–12 minutes until the biscuits are golden brown. Using a spatula, transfer the biscuits to a wire rack to cool completely before serving.

Nutty Flapjacks

INGREDIENTS

200 g/7 oz rolled oats

115 g/4 oz chopped hazelnuts

55 g/2 oz plain flour

115 g/4 oz butter, plus extra for greasing

2 tbsp golden syrup

85 g/3 oz light muscovado sugar

makes 16

1 Preheat the oven to 180°C/350°F/Gas Mark 4, then grease a 23-cm/9-inch square cake tin. Place the rolled oats, chopped hazelnuts and flour in a large mixing bowl and stir together.

2 Place the butter, golden syrup and sugar in a saucepan over a low heat and stir until melted. Pour onto the dry ingredients and mix well. Turn the mixture into the prepared tin and smooth the surface with the back of a spoon.

3 Bake in the preheated oven for 20–25 minutes, or until golden and firm to the touch. Mark into 16 pieces and leave to cool in the tin. When completely cooled, cut through with a sharp knife and remove from the tin.

Marshmallow Float

INGREDIENTS

serves ❹

225 g/8 oz plain chocolate, broken into pieces

900 ml/1½ pints milk

3 tbsp caster sugar

8 marshmallows

1 Finely chop the chocolate with a knife or in a food processor. Do not over-process or the chocolate will melt.

2 Pour the milk into a saucepan and bring to just below boiling point. Remove the saucepan from the heat and whisk in the sugar and the chocolate.

3 Pour into heatproof glasses, top each with two marshmallows and serve immediately.

Index